BRITAIN IN OLD PHOTOGRAPHS

KENDAL REVISITED

MARGARET & PERCY DUFF

SUTTON PUBLISHING LIMITED

Sutton Publishing Limited
Phoenix Mill · Thrupp · Stroud
Gloucestershire · GL5 2BU

First published 1997

Reprinted in 2002

Cover photographs: *front*: Street market in
Stramongate, 1950s; *back*; Mr and Mrs Edward
Boundy, keen motorists.

British Library Cataloguing in Publication Data
A catalogue record for this book is available from the
British Library.

ISBN 0-7509-1508-0

Typeset in 10/12 Perpetua.
Typesetting and origination by
Sutton Publishing Limited.
Printed in Great Britain by
J. H. Haynes & Co. Ltd, Sparkford.

CONTENTS

The Kendal Coat of Arms in the garden at Nether Bridge. The arms were first used in 1629.

INTRODUCTION

This is the second book of old photographs based on a collection we have made relating to the ancient town of Kendal, the largest and most important in the former County of Westmorland, which has long been known as 'The Gateway to the Lakes'. It is the centre for the surrounding, mainly agricultural, community and the annual Westmorland County Show held just south of the town is one of the oldest in the country.

The prosperity of the town was founded on the woollen industry, which flourished for several centuries. 'Kendal Green', a heavy woollen cloth, became famous for its hard-wearing quality, and Shakespeare immortalized it in his *Henry IV*. A large export trade developed to America and the West Indies. The importance of this industry to Kendal has dwindled with the passing of the years and the coming of the Industrial Revolution. Its place has been taken by other industries: K Shoes; snuff and tobacco, water turbines and pumps; paper; and carpets, all of which were established in the nineteenth century. More recently, the world famous Kendal Mintcake has been regarded as essential on many expeditions and was eaten by Hillary and Tenzing on the top of the world when they conquered Everest.

The difficulties of transport were of course an obstacle to rapid development. In early times the woollen goods were distributed throughout the country and to various ports for export by packhorse. The town grew more quickly when the canal arrived. The Town Council, with considerable forethought, had purchased the land at Canal Head where the canal from Preston was to terminate. It also built Miller Bridge in 1818 to improve the access from the town. The canal prospered until the arrival of the railway in 1846, when trade was moved to this speedier form of transport. These days the M6 and the West Coast main railway line make Kendal an ideal centre for commerce, and easily accessible to tourists.

The River Kent, which flows through the centre of the town, is one of the shortest and fastest-flowing in England. Until the 1970s, winter floods were a regular occurence, but a major improvement scheme has been very successful, and riverside residents and shopkeepers have not been troubled since that time.

The castle on the hill was never the scene of any warlike activity and has gradually fallen into disrepair. For some time this has been a cause for concern, but a major scheme is now under way to save and make safe what remains of the castle's ancient walls.

The parish church of the Holy Trinity in Kirkland, built in the Gothic style, dates from the thirteenth century and was built on the site of an earlier church. Unusual in having five aisles, it is one of the largest churches in England. It contains the colours of the 55th Regiment of Foot raised in 1755, which together with the 34th became the Border Regiment in 1881.

Kendal is a growing town and, unfortunately, its main streets, like those of many other old market towns, are gradually losing their character. Shop fronts in particular are being standardized like those throughout the rest of the country.

This nostalgic collection of photographs illustrates some of the changes and great occasions that have taken place over the last century.

We acknowledge with thanks the permission granted by the editor of the *Westmorland Gazette* to use the following photographs: 17 upper, 29, 46 lower, 85 (both) and 106 lower.

Looking from Highgate into Stricklandgate at the end of the nineteenth century.

RECREATION

Kendal Borough Band outside Abbot Hall, early 1920s. Unfortunately this band no longer exists, so the bands of the Sea Cadets and Boys Brigade now lead civic parades.

The 'K' Fete, Netherfield Cricket Field, Parkside Road, 1939. The 'K' Queen, Barbara Airey, has just been crowned. With her are her attendants and her escort, Leonard Robinson.

The council dust cart with an escort of girls from the K Shoe Factory on Aynam Road in the 'K' Fete Procession. 'Bringing Back The Ashes' refers to the test matches being played at the time with Australia.

Westmorland Motor Club members on a social run at the top of Kirkstone Pass, just after the First World War. Those sitting on motor cycles are, from left to right: Billy Westwood, Guy Jefferys, Bryan Jefferys, Will Hutchinson, Stan Bewsher and Dick Chaplow. Kit Parker is standing on the far right.

The Foden Steam Wagon from Levens Hall taking part in the Torchlight Procession, 1973. Those in the cab, from left to right, are: Ron Thompson, Ken Jackson and Hal Bagot (owner).

The Zion Church Drama Group present *Quiet Night*, 1957. The nurses seated at the tables are Alice Park (left) and Dorothy Howie (right).

YWCA Pioneers netball team, November 1935. This Kendal team won the netball competition at the Albert Hall on the occasion of the YWCA eightieth birthday celebrations.

Kendal rugby team, 30 April 1932. These were the winners of the Manchester Rugby seven-a-side competition. Back row, left to right: Jack Beck, Jackie Morris, Pat Morris, Alec Johnson and Billy Holland. Front row: Paddy Murdock, Sammy Martindale and Bram Storey.

Kendal Rugby Union Football Club, 1952/3 season. Back row, left to right: John Blades, Brian Ferguson, Hilton Elliott, Stuart Davidson, Joe Robinson, Alan Stables, Harry Hall, George Goff and Paddy Murdock. Middle row: Malcolm Turner, Bruce Reed, Myers Ferguson, Arthur Oates and Bobby Hogg. Front row: Derek Sharpe and Geoff Todhunter.

Publicity leaflet for the Victorian Academy of Dancing. The room pictured is now used by the Red Cross.

Daffodil Girls of the Victorian Academy of Dancing, 1911. Left to right: Annie Noble, Moya Docherty, Eva Monkhouse, Marjorie Braithwaite, Beatrice Greenbank and Marjorie Noble.

The Mary Wakefield Westmorland Festival. The festival was founded in 1885. Mary Wakefield, the founder, is on the far left with one of the competing string orchestras. The motto of the festival is 'Music is a fair and glorious gift of God'.

West Lancashire League Cup semi-final, Parkside Road, 1938/9. The score was Netherfield 8, Lancaster CMH nil. Back row, left to right: G.C. Jones, J. McKendry, R. Stuart, D. Gilpin, J. Crooks, W. Remington and R. Brennand. Front row: E. Wilson, J. Clarke, Joe Hillbeck, G. Bellas, J. Knagg (Capt.), W. Hutton, D. Ward, A. Sutton and R. Rigg.

Kendal Cricket Club with the North Lancashire League Cup, 1947. Back row (committee), left to right: H. Howson, F.R. Stewart, W. Porter, G. Ellwood, T. Richardson and R. Roberts. Middle row: H. Dalzell, H. Morgan, A. Corless, P. Greenwood, G. Sibley, W. Harrison and J. Richardson. Front row: B. Reed, F.T. Long, A. Johnson (Capt.), R.S. Ellwood and A.J. Leggatt.

Girl Guides in the mini skirt era of the 1960s on Mayor's Sunday, passing the Town Hall. Miss Marjorie Dinsdale and Miss Edith Mounsey are in the lead.

The 2nd Kendal Guide Company leaving Kendal for a rally at Appleby Castle, 27 May 1922.

Miss England II in Kirkland on the way to Windermere, June 1930. Sir Henry Seagrave was killed while attempting to break the water speed record.

The drums and bugles, together with a full parade of the 1st Kendal Boy Scouts, *c.* 1938.

K Shoes choir in the Assembly Room in the Town Hall, 1930s. Apart from the guest artists in the centre of the front row, all of those present were employed at the K Shoes factory.

Kendal Amateur Operatic Society. The society was formed in 1913 and its first show was *Iolanthe*. The whole cast assembled behind Hogg's Studio in Stricklandgate for this photograph.

Customers of the Rifleman's Arms about to set off on their annual outing in a Ribble bus driven by Sam Ellwood.

The YMCA billiard team with the Riley Challenge Shield. Before the Second World War the YMCA had premises above shops nos 24 and 26 Stricklandgate. Back row, left to right: Joe Rigg, Doug Todd, Jack Lightburn (later editor of the *Westmorland Gazette*) and George Graham. Front row: Albert Duxbury, Jimmy Lewis and John Simpson.

TRANSPORT

Kendal Corporation drivers with their horse-drawn carts. The council depot at this time was in the old stable block at Abbot Hall, with an entrance from Kirkland down Peppercorn Lane.

The *Royal Scot* starting to climb the bank, just north of Oxenholme Station, early 1930s. The train engine is a parallel boilered unidentified Royal Scot Class. The pilot engine is a former London and North Western Railway Whale Precursor 4–4–0 Oceanic.

A train of empty wagons hauled by a 4–6–0 Black Five climbing the bank to Oxenholme adjoining Castle Road. James Cropper's paper mills at Burneside had coal-fired boilers and received regular supplies by rail. These were taken from Burneside Station on their private line, hauled by their own engine.

Rebuilt Patriot 45537 waiting at Oxenholme before proceeding down the branch line to Kendal and Windermere. The branch is now served by a two-car diesel unit.

The King's Arms Hotel bus waiting at Kendal Station. On the left is the driver, Alf Ward, who later started his own taxi business. The porter on the right is Tommy Garnett.

The Westmorland County Council steamroller working at Castle Green Lane. This road was widened in March 1956. The driver is Matthew James.

Westmorland County Council steamrollers, Mint Bridge, early 1930s. The bridge was being widened and was tested by a fleet of these steamrollers.

Horse-drawn delivery van, Maude Street. William Hartley, baker and confectioner, had a shop at 112 Stricklandgate, now an estate agent. He had another shop in Mercer's Lane, which formed one side of the present market-place.

One of Rutter's coaches on New Road at the bottom of Kent Street.

Car delivered to Herbert John Croft in 1905. Croft was a cycle dealer at 1 Wildman Street at the end of the nineteenth century, but he was quick to move into motor cars and become an agent for such well-known makes as Humber, Rover and Daimler. Later he moved into premises at 84–92 Highgate and was an agent for Austin, Morris and Rover cars. Jeans are now sold in the former showroom.

A competitor in the Automobile Club 1000-mile Trial, 1 May 1900. He receives a warm welcome as he approaches Kendal. The car is a 6 hp Panhard manufactured by Messrs Panhard et Levassor, Paris. The owner was F.H. Butler.

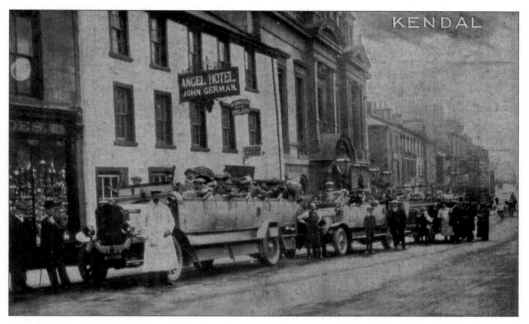

Charabanc parties from Morecambe, calling for lunch at the Angel Hotel before proceeding on a tour of the Lake District.

F.W. Stainton and Son are coach hire specialists and operate both British and continental tours. Mr Stainton is at the wheel of an early charabanc.

Paul Rochard on his Ariel Twin Combination outside the Catholic Church on New Road, 1923.

Mr and Mrs Edward Boundy, who lived in Wildman Street and were keen motorists. Mr Boundy was an early car dealer and had premises in Yard 56, Stramongate.

Z. Crabtree and Co. adjoining Atkinson & Griffin, Kirkland, 1930s. There was keen competition at this time to catch the passing traffic on its way to the Lake District. This property is now the Renault showrooms and no longer operates as a garage.

The market-place before the Second World War. The attendant is making sure that no car is out of line. This area has since been pedestrianized.

Todd & Leggett taking delivery of an early caterpillar tractor at the company's premises in Sandes Avenue. These premises are now occupied by a firm of tyre dealers. Across the road is a small garage owned by William O'Loughlin. This was demolished and replaced by a car park.

Alf Burrow with his removal van at the entrance to Maude Street. Note the early road sign for Carlisle.

COMMERCE & INDUSTRY

The 'new' press being installed in the Gazette's press hall, 1934. The Mayor, Councillor Knowles, has his hand on the switch.

Staff at the Kendal steam laundry in Wildman Street taking a break. Standing, left to right: Nellie Dobson, Maggie Grant, Evelyn Green and Fanny Graham. Sitting: Edith Coulton, Jessie Graham and Edith Brennand.

Mill girls outside the carpet factory, Highgate. This factory was destroyed by fire. All work is now concentrated at Castle Mills on Aynam Road, which is owned by Goodacres Carpets Ltd.

Mill girls at Braithwaites woollen mill, Mealbank, *c.* 1894. Braithwaites also had a mill in Highgate.

Girls at work in the steam laundry, Wildman Street.

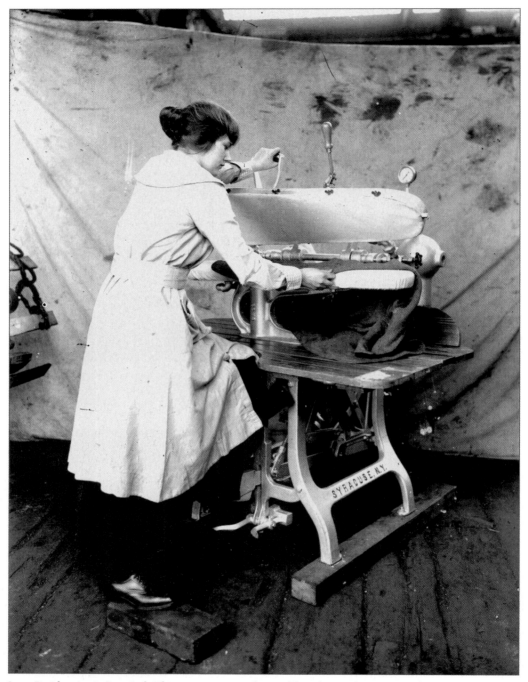

Isaac Braithwaite & Sons Ltd. This company manufactured laundry machinery at its factory in Ann Street and also supplied Hoffman presses under licence. This girl is working a Hoffman press. Note 'Syracuse NY' on the stand. In 1925 the firm moved to premises on Shap Road. The company's trade mark was 'IBIS'.

Girls working in the laundry in Ann Street.

Isaac Braithwaite's workmen at the Ann Street factory.

The Saturday market in Stramongate where farmer's wives were allowed to sell their produce from wheeled carts. Stalls were not allowed. The canopy over the entrance to St George's Hall is in the background.

The annual Damson Saturday Market, Highgate. Nowadays, farm carts have given way on this thoroughfare through the town to two streams of traffic following the one-way system.

Street market in Stramongate, 1950s. It is still a legal requirement to sell from wheeled vehicles, but the old carts have given way to car boots and trailers.

The fish market, which used to be held at the top of Finkle Street. This site is now occupied by a glass and steel shelter, very much out of keeping with the surrounding buildings.

Jordan's granary at the junction of Beast Banks and Low Fellside. The building, built in 1888, was demolished in 1971 to improve the junction and to make access to the development at High Fellside.

The coaching staff at the rear of the King's Arms Hotel.

Decorated float behind the houses in Ann Street. The float is displaying IBIS laundry machinery.

Horse-drawn cart belonging to J.J. & W. Wilson outside the company's mill on Aynam Road. J.J. & W. Wilson Ltd was in business at Castle Mills from 1853 after buying the mill from the borough council for £5,000. The company specialized in travelling rugs and tweeds, some of which can be seen on the cart.

Staff of the Stockbeck tannery look on as W. Woodburn's men paint the outside of the factory. The property is now occupied by Earnshaw's suite centre.

Stockbeck tannery. The firm was operated by William and John Little, who can be seen standing at the gate to the tannery, with employees Jack Friend and Ned Troughton on their left.

THE SERVICES

Kendal Borough special constables outside Abbot Hall, 1940. The Mayor, Alderman 'Billy' Cleasby, is in the centre. On his left are the chief constable Pat O'Neil and S.T. Clarke. On his right are Percy Hastewell and Terence O'Brien.

The Kings Own Royal Border Regiment marching past the town hall on the occasion of the tercentenary parade, 11 June 1980.

The civic party at the town hall. Those present include Councillor Vic Hadley, Mayor of Kendal, and Councillor Abel Ward, chairman of the South Lakeland District Council.

The 4th (Territorial) Battalion, the Border Regiment, marching behind their drum and fife band to the parish church to 'lay up' their colours on the first Sunday in September 1939. Many of these men were taken prisoner on the retreat to Dunkirk.

'D' Company of the 4th Battalion, the Border Regiment, on Kendal Station forecourt before leaving by train on mobilization, September 1939. This battalion landed in France on 17 November 1939, being one of the first TA infantry units to serve overseas.

The ladies of the Civil Defence with Inspector Herbert Wilson, 1940.

Gas drill with Sergeant Herbert Wilson (prior to his promotion to inspector), 1939.

Heavy rescue squads for civil defence were trained at the old Gunpowder Works at Gatebeck. These courses were organized by Westmorland County Council.

The Volunteer Fire Brigade outside its station on Aynam Road, before taking part in the Peace Celebrations Procession, 19 July 1919.

The colour party of the 4th Battalion, the Border Regiment, leading a parade down Highgate to the parish church. Before the Second World War it was the practice for the newly elected Mayor to invite local associations to accompany him to church for the annual civic service.

The motor cycle despatch riders of the local Home Guard battalion of the Border Regiment. Note the pudding basin helmets and the masks on the headlights.

Local volunteers from the St John Ambulance Brigade, who helped to staff the hospital in Stramongate for soldiers wounded in the First World War.

Kendal Division of the St John Ambulance Brigade, 1936. The division was under the command of Colonel Cockill.

The Border Regiment receives the freedom of the Borough of Kendal, October 1947. In line in front of the Mayor, Walter Wilkinson, are the Arroyo drummers. Their drums were captured from the French at Arroyo dos Molinos on 28 October 1811.

Kendal Sea Cadet Corps, outside Castle Street School, 1940. The physical training instructor is Steve Pickthall.

Volunteers who formed the Kendal Pals Battalion in the First World War, assembled in Kendal before leaving for training.

The survivors of the Old Comrades Association of the 25th Division, who fought in France in the First World War, parade past the cenotaph behind their chairman, Billy Ellwood, *c.* 1950.

Kendal Pals in the trenches, 15 July 1916. The 8th Battalion, the Border Regiment, was deployed on the Somme at Ovillers.

SHOPS & INNS

*R.W. and T.K. Thompson's premises on the corner of Finkle Street and Branthwaite Brow. This establishment was **the** gents outfitters. The staff are surrounded by a special display of summer headgear, all at 1s (5p).*

Wilsons is one of the famous Kendal Mintcake manufacturers. It now has its premises in Cross Lane. This shop has been incorporated into the new Black Hall Yard shopping precinct.

Mrs Cooper and her son at the door of their shop on Serpentine Road.

These premises are now the Highgate Hotel. There has been a hotel on this site since 1769.

The County Hotel, 1915. Originally it was called the Railway and Commercial Hotel because of its situation on Station Road. What was Mr Smith's tobacconists is now part of the hotel.

Whitwell, Mark & Co. Ltd's brewery, Highgate. The brewery is decorated for the coronation of King George V. This part of the building is now the YHA Hostel. The buildings to the rear have been converted into an arts centre.

The Hyena Inn, Fountain Brow. This inn was not demolished when Fellside was cleared but was converted for residential use. Adjoining it are typical Fellside cottages.

Bargains in Men's Clothing.

IMPERIA SUITS AND OVERCOATS
at Sale Prices.

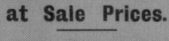

A golden opportunity of trying this famous brand of clothing.

Every garment bears the Imperia trade=mark and guarantee. Only a limited number to be sold at these low prices.

Don't delay or you will miss them.

	USUAL PRICE.	SALE PRICE.
OVERCOATS	37/6	30/-
SUITS - -	35/6	26/6

Men's Suits & Overcoats
Ordinary Makes, from **15/11**

Bargains in Juvenile Clothing.

Now is the time to fit your boys up with a good school "rig=out" at a moderate price. Good sound Suits. Those that will stand any amount of rough wear.

Come and have a look at them.

		SALE PRICE
Youths' Trouser Suits from		12/6 to 22/6
„ Knicker „ „		9/3 to 20/-
Boy's Sailor „ „		1/11 to 11/6
„ Belted „ „		4/11 to 13/6
„ Norfolk „ „		4/11 to 17/6

A few odd Jackets, Vests and Knickers to clear cheap

Sale poster, 1910. There were some interesting bargains at Blacow's sale.

Blacow's hatters, hosiers and outfitters, Finkle Street, 1909. In the following year the shop was set back in line with other properties in Finkle Street. This family business, which was established in 1772, continues today in the Westmorland shopping centre.

Row of shops, Stricklandgate, 1930s. Townley & Taylor was the local agent for Meccano sets and Hornby trains. In addition it specialized in prams and baby carriages. All of these properties have been demolished. W.H. Smith moved from a small shop near the town hall to a much larger store on the site formerly occupied by Jim Bird. A Co-op supermarket occupied the other site for some time, followed by NORWEB. It is now New Look ladies fashions.

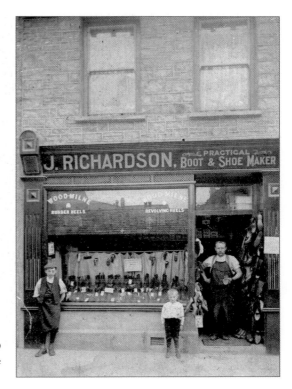

Mr Richardson at the door of his shop at 19 Wildman Street. G.J. Moore, rope and twine manufacturer, moved in after Mr Richardson.

Stramongate, looking north. William Henry Hiscox was at 1 Stramongate and sold stationery, fancy goods and typewriter supplies. Later this shop was occupied by Stubbs & Co. ladies' outfitters, baby linen and children's wear. In 1996 it changed hands to become Johnsons the cleaners.

Mrs Townley at the door of her family's bakery at 81 Highgate, 1904. Later this shop was taken over by Gould & Heywood, electricians. Now it is occupied by Raymond Wightman, watchmaker and jewellers.

The corner of Finkle Street and Kent Street. S. Heap, who had a shop here, described himself as a furnishing ironmonger. The premises later became Kendal Corporation's electricity department's showrooms. They are now part of J.R. Taylor's store.

Two elegant customers leaving Braithwaite's café on the corner of Stramongate and Branthwaite Brow. This shop is now David Kerr, gents' outfitter.

The Commercial Room in the Waverley Temperance Hotel, Stramongate, 1912.

Adjoining shops in Highgate occupied by James Capstick, a tailor, and Richard Beetham, a greengrocer. Now with modern shop fronts they house a financial advisor and Soutergate Gallery.

The Dolphin Refreshment Rooms, Highgate, on the corner of Allhallows Lane. These were converted into a shop for Thompsons, which sold glass and china. The premises are now occupied by Kneed the Dough.

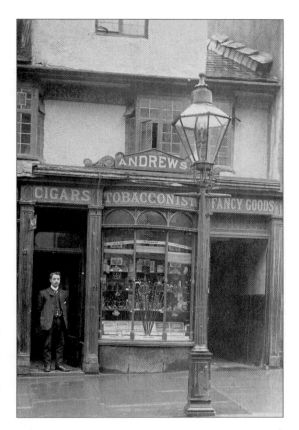

Mr Andrew at the door of his shop at 26 Highgate, 1906. Previously this business had been owned by G. Ireland. The shop next door was occupied by T. Wilson, printer, stationer and lithographer. This was the first shop in Kendal to have electric light. Later, Titus Wilson combined the two premises.

The King's Arms Hotel, Stricklandgate, prior to 1936. The hotel bus is at the entrance, but the bedrooms were over the adjoining shops.

Webb's Commercial Hotel, which was demolished when Black Hall Road was extended from Stramongate to New Road.

Harrisons, 82–6 Stramongate. This was one of the larger grocers in town. Builders Supply used the premises as showrooms before moving into Wildman Street. The building is now occupied by Proffitts House furnishers.

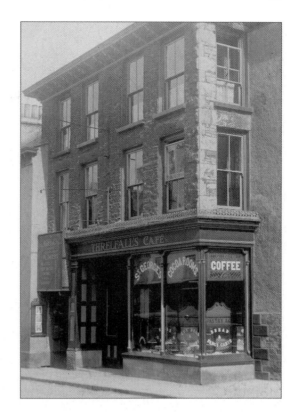

Threlfall's café, Stramongate. This was a favourite meeting place for the farmers on market days. It was affectionately known as 'St George's Cocoa Rooms'. The building was demolished when Black Hall Road was extended from Stramongate to New Road.

Kendal Co-operative Society shop, Sandylands Road. The Co-operative Society had several shops in the town, as well as branches in the surrounding villages. This wooden store has long since disappeared, together with the Kendal Society. The poster advertises a free exhibition in the market hall.

The former King's Arms Hotel. The hotel ceased to trade in 1936. The shop frontage was set back, and both Burtons and Marks & Spencer arrived in Kendal.

The reception area in the King's Arms Hotel.

Daniel Quiggin's shop, 86 Stricklandgate. Quiggin also had a shop at 25 Allhallows Lane. His advertisement said: 'Our sweets are warranted pure and of the finest quality. Try them!'

Quiggin's shop on the corner of Allhallows Lane and Highgate, 1929. Doris Bean and Mary Wilson are at the door.

The New Shambles, leading from the market-place to Finkle Street.

The Borough Band conducted by John May, playing carols outside the Fleece Inn, Christmas 1938.

Two bar maids at the Roebuck, 1897. At this time the entrance was up yard 50, Highgate.

Highgate before Woolworths came to Kendal, early 1930s. Woolworths purchased the two shops in the centre of this picture.

The Seven Stars Hotel, Stricklandgate. This hotel sold Younger's Ales, hence the sign: 'Get Younger Here'. This building was demolished and has been replaced by the entrance to the Black Hall shopping arcade.

Daniel Quiggin's shop at 25 Allhallows Lane.

J. & J.T. Smith, jewellers, 1a Highgate. This shop was subsequently occupied by Fred Long as a tobacconist and was a mecca for the local rugby and cricket players. Long was a good all-round sportsman, and he captained Kendal Cricket Club and Kendal Rugby Club when in his prime. This small shop has now been incorporated into the shop next door.

A banquet, ready for the county ball at the Commercial Hotel, *c.* 1900.

Joe Booth's sweet and tobacco shop, 3 Kirkland.

Raffles Antiques, Wildman Street. These premises were formerly an old Kendal farmhouse.

SECTION SIX

STREET SCENES

Proud Fellsiders at the junction of Fountain Brow and Fell Brow with Sepulchre Lane. In spite of overcrowding and poor public services, every effort was made to keep the cottages clean.

A typical Fellside family. Fellside was a tough community, but the hard life bred a sense of belonging, friendship and mutual help in times of need.

No. 11 Fountain Brow. Note the WC lean-to outbuilding extending on to the pavement.

Children playing in Fountain Brow.

Washing day at 1 Cliff Lane. Allhallows church is in the background.

J.W. Carlisle's warehouse. It was demolished along with the adjoining property to make way for extensions to the Provincial insurance company's offices.

Two early cyclists, Rosemary Lane. The lane connected Stramongate with the River Kent. When the car park was constructed and the lane was widened, the name was changed to New Road. The building in the foreground was demolished and Melrose Place was built in its place.

The Old Shambles. Richardson's barrel and churn works are in the background. The buildings on the left are now part of the Fleece Inn. On the right is Alexander's the wine merchants, which is now an insurance broker's office.

Caroline Street residents. This part of the street was also known as Malt Kiln Hill.

The Sleddalls Almshouses, Aynam Road. The almshouses were erected in 1887 by John Sleddall to the honour and glory of God for the succour and protection of worthy inhabitants of the Borough of Kendal in commemoration of Queen Victoria's Golden Jubilee. The chapel at the end of the terrace was built for the benefit of those who lived there. It has now been converted into residential accommodation.

Castle Mills. The Skew Bridge on Aynam Road was removed when Castle Mills no longer used water power. The mill race was filled in and the road straightened.

Farmers and their wives in Stramongate preparing for the market.

Hiring day for farm workers, Whit Saturday, 1903. The farmers and workers congregated between the market-place and the top of Finkle Street.

The high arch of the Woolpack Hotel. This arch was necessary to allow the hooped carts carrying wool to pass from Stricklandgate up Woolpack Yard.

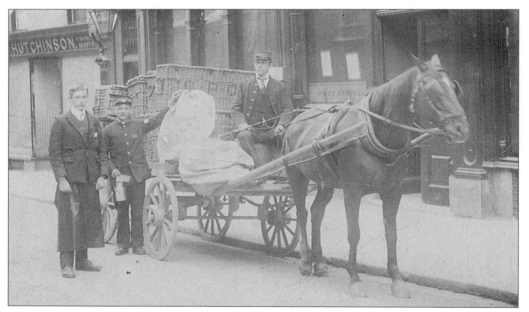

Horse-drawn mail delivery. At the turn of the century the mail arrived by the 5.00 a.m. train of the London and North Western Railway at Kendal Station. It was brought to the post office in Finkle Street by this horse-drawn cart. The postmaster at the time was William Francis Duff, the author's grandfather.

Dowker and Wilson's charity provided six dwellings for 'females of good and chaste character born in the town of Kendal having obtained fifty years of age'. The charity was founded in 1831 with a bequest from Miss Dorothy Dowker of £3,000. The cottages were demolished together with the entrance gate to Abbot Hall to make an entrance to the South East Highgate dwellings and car park. The new street was named Dowker's Lane. The front arch is preserved in Webster's Yard in Highgate.

Highgate before the arrival of the motor car. Crossing the road would not be so leisurely today, with traffic backing up from the town hall traffic lights.

Stricklandgate, with the local children from the yards playing safely in the street. There were no planning restrictions on shop signs. The large chimneys belong to the Strickland's Town House.

A similar view to that above, 1930s. The shops have not altered to any great extent but the Strickland Town House is now the general post office.

ROYAL & CIVIC OCCASIONS

YWCA centenary celebrations, 2 July 1960. The new club building was opened by HRH Princess Alice, Countess of Athlone.
Those present include Mrs Worsdell (president), Princess Alice and the Lord Lieutenant, Mr Hornyold Strickland.

Civic service in the parish church on the occasion of the YWCA centenary celebrations. HRH Princess Alice is with the Lord Lieutenant. The vicar is Canon Bertram Jones.

Mayor's Sunday parade, late 1930s. Kendal Borough Chief Constable Pat O'Neil is followed by PS Herbert Wilson and PC Wilf Miller. The volunteer Fire Brigade is also represented.

Lady Mountbatten and Dr George Edgecombe arriving at the headquarters of the Kendal St John Ambulance Brigade, 1943.

Lady Mountbatten in the St John Ambulance room with members of the brigade, the Mayor and other civic dignitaries.

A street party in the Lound to celebrate Queen Elizabeth's coronation. In the background is the sanatorium for infectious diseases, which was converted into flats after the Second World War.

Street party at Rinkfield to celebrate the coronation of Queen Elizabeth, 1952.

Civic parade to the war memorial for the Remembrance Day Service, 1946. In the centre are, left to right: Alderman T.H. Dobie (deputy Mayor), Alderman Walter Wilkinson (Mayor) and Harold Rhodes (town clerk). The mace bearers are PCs Eric Parkinson and Jim Little.

The Civic Party at the war memorial in the market-place, November 1934. In front are, left to right: Councillor Ernest Jones (deputy Mayor), John Knowles (Mayor) and Harold Rhodes (town clerk). Sergeant L. Heap is carrying the sword and PC Herbert Wilson is holding the mace.

Old People's Welfare Centre, opening ceremony, 3 September 1964. Left to right: Jack Coward (builder), the Revd B. Jones (vicar of Kendal), Mrs Mildred Stables, Brian Dockray, Mrs Anna Shaw (Mayoress), Charlie Dent, John Shaw (Mayor), Peter Scott, Alderman Knowles and Mrs Knowles.

The Old Folks Treat, 1947. This event has been held annually for more than 100 years. The Mayor (Alderman Wilkinson) and the Mayoress, together with the chairman (Alderman Bruce Alexander) are among those present. For many years, Kendal Co-operative Society catered for this event and the staff from the various branches waited at the tables.

Queen Elizabeth II leaving County Hall on the occasion of her official visit, 11 August 1956. On the left are the Mayor and Mayoress of Kendal, Councillor and Mrs Billy Gould, who had previously welcomed the royal visitor to the town hall.

Waiting for the Queen outside the County Hall, August 1956.

The Women's Voluntary Services and the Civil Defence Corps line the forecourt of the County Hall waiting for the Queen. The stand was for representatives of the religious, social, cultural and business life of the county.

Princess Alexandra leaves Queen Katherine School with the Lord Lieutenant, Paul Wilson, 25 March 1976. The Princess opened the College of Further Education and the Folk Museum at Abbot Hall.

Crowd outside the town hall waiting to hear the Mayor read the Royal Proclamation from the historic 'Call Stone', 9 February 1952. Locally known as the 'Ca Steean' it formed the base of the ancient market cross which originally stood in Stricklandgate. It has been used for the proclamation of successive monarchs of England from time immemorial.

Procession to celebrate the coronation of Queen Elizabeth II. The float of the Kendal Sea Cadet Corps is just passing the town hall.

Visit of Princess Christian on the occasion of the twenty-first Mary Wakefield Westmorland Festival, 1906. After calling at the town hall, the Princess proceeded along Aynam Road to the drill hall, where the festival was being held. This stand was erected for the children.

Crowds in Stricklandgate, August 1891. This occasion was the Arts, Crafts and Loan Exhibition, which was opened by HRH Princess Louise. It included this procession of horse-drawn exhibits round the town.

The town hall, decorated for Queen Victoria's Golden Jubilee, 1887. The adjoining property was purchased and the town hall was extended in time for the Queen's Diamond Jubilee, when the carillon was inaugurated.

Decorations at the top of Finkle Street celebrating the coronation of King George V. The occupiers of the shops have changed and the shop fronts have been modernized, but the Liberal Club remains the same.

Their Royal Highnesses the Duke and Duchess of York at the K Shoe Factory, April 1935.

EDUCATION & RELIGION

The Wesleyan Methodist Chapel at the junction of Burneside Road and Windermere Road. It was rebuilt in 1882 on the site of the original chapel, which had been erected in 1808. The gates and railings were removed during the Second World War. The bodies in the burial ground were removed to Parkside Road Cemetery when the entrance to Burneside Road was widened after the war.

Castle Street School String Orchestra. This school was closed shortly after the Second World War.

St George's School infants, 1924/5. The teacher is Miss Mason. This school is now the Masonic Hall.

Sande Aire Sunday School children on an outing in the fields at Sparrowmire, 1946.

Sunday School children in procession in Stricklandgate celebrating the coronation of Queen Elizabeth II, June 1953.

Dalton Houses at Thorney Hills (upper) and Sedbergh Road (lower). Stramongate School was a boys school under the control of the Friends in Kendal. Although it had space for 40 day boys, the majority of the pupils were boarders and were accommodated in three boarding houses. There were eight resident masters and two resident mistresses.

Children's Sports, Abbot Hall Park. The sports were held annually for more than a century and there was keen competition between the schools. The children also gave displays of formation dancing and Maypole dancing, which attracted large crowds of parents.

Kendal Green School cricket team, 1920s. At this time there was no money to spare for cricket whites, but these players are happy in their ordinary clothes.

Kendal Green School football team, 1921/2. William Gardiner, the headmaster, is on the left. The goalkeeper is Jack Wilson of the Kendal Mintcake Wilson family.

Sandylands Methodist Church, 1953. The church was extended and the foundation stone was laid by Mrs Thomas Pearson in the presence of the Mayor and Mayoress (Councillor Tom and Mrs O'Loughlin) and the Revd Robert Armstrong.

The ladies of St George's Church taking tea at their Country Fair, 13 August 1910. Castle Hill is in the background.

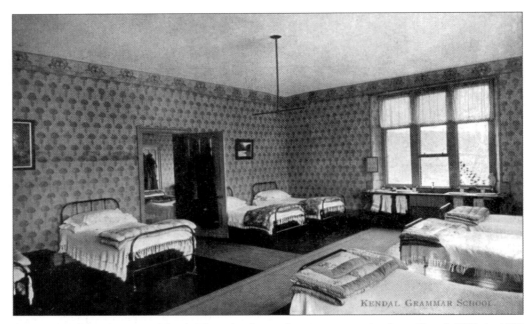

Dormitory of the Grammar School. This school moved to its present site from Church Walk in 1889 when it was opened by the Lord Mayor of London, Sir James Whitehead, who had come to Kendal to receive the Freedom of the Borough. Before the Second World War the school encouraged boarders.

The Open Air Art Class at the Grammar School. It would be interesting to see the drawings by the boys who could only see the horse's hindquarters!

St Thomas' Church. This church was built in 1836 at a cost of £3,000. This is a busy junction where Stricklandgate joins Windermere Road and Burneside Road. The railings and the lamp have long since disappeared and the road has been widened. A modern extension for parish activities has been built adjoining the church where the trees are.

The Inghamite Chapel. This chapel was built in 1844 on the site of the Old Meeting House, which had been converted into a chapel in 1750. The building has now been converted into flats.

The Salvation Army Hall was in Black Hall Yard above L. Airey & Co., plumbers. This whole area has been cleared and the Salvation Army now meets in Gillinggate Mission Hall.

The Kendal Salvation Army Band, 1951.

FLOODS & PUBLIC WORKS

Floods of 1954. These were the highest floods since 1927. Outside the Provincial head offices the road rapidly became impassable.

Looking from Sandes Avenue towards Stramongate Bridge, when the record flood of 1898 nearly filled the bridge arches.

Looking south down the Waterside, when the 1898 flood was at its highest.

Floods of November 1927. These floods closed Kirkland, when the culvert under the road was unable to contain Brockbeck. A 'K' bus can be seen waiting to come into town.

Floods of November 1898. These floods demolished the Jenning's Yard Footbridge, which connected the Waterside with Aynam Road.

Washerwomen outside the public baths and wash-houses in Allhallows Lane. John Hodgkinson, the caretaker, is on the left.

Swimming bath, Allhallows Lane. The swimming bath was added to the baths and washhouses in 1884, when they were purchased by the borough council from a private company. It was 60 ft by 30 ft, and there were five private baths and a laundry. The property is now known as Shearman House and is used as offices by the South Lakeland District Council.

Castle Street at the beginning of the twentieth century, when the borough council was actively engaged in installing a comprehensive sewage system throughout the town. The high standard of timber shoring of the trenches obviously met with the approval of the borough surveyor.

Floods of 1927. These floods caused considerable damage, and the pressure of water demolished the wall and railings on New Road.

Road lowering under Longpool railway bridge. Kendal Borough Council, as agents for the Ministry of Transport, made arrangements for the road to be lowered under the Longpool railway bridge. At that time the A6 was the main route to the North. The M6 now deals with all of the heavy traffic. Previously, high loads had to be diverted. The main contractor was W.H. Ainsworth. Note the council steamroller in action.

A MISCELLANY

The Staff of the Kendal Borough treasurer's department, 1966. Back row, left to right. Ron Wheatman, Roger Wilson, Ralph Cannon and Harry Long. Middle row: Rose Fallowes, Harry Robinson, Tony Johnson, Allen Crossley, Susan Seed, Chris Patrick, Ronnie Moorby and Mary Ratcliffe. Front row: Margaret Stewart, Gerald Procter, Alfred Wainwright, Percy Duff and Kathleen Thompson.

The Common Lodging House on the Waterside, 1959. This building was demolished to make way for the south-east Highgate housing development.

The Midland Bank, Highgate, 1906. The railings and window-boxes have disappeared, but the lion still occupies pride of place above the main entrance.

The Castle Estate VE Day party, Netherfield Sports Ground.

Children in the Co-operative Jubilee Parade crossing Miller Bridge, 1912. The parade finished in Town View field, where the children were given refreshments.

The Provincial insurance company's staff party, 22 December 1943.

Kendal Auction Mart, *c.* 1938. A shorthorn cow is in the ring with Harold Hodgson, auctioneer. The Auction Mart company directors sat with the auctioneer.

Judging the fancy dress in Abbot Hall Park during holidays at Home Week, 1945. The Mayor, Alderman T.H. Dobie, is accompanied by his wife and Tommy Atkinson.

These are the children who entered the fancy dress competition.

A young motorist in the Lound having his number taken, probably for failing his MOT!

Children on Serpentine Road, 1913.

YWCA centenary celebrations (1860–1960). At the table as the birthday cake is cut are, left to right: Mrs Milly Stables, Mrs E.M. Worsdell, Mrs B. Whitwell (Mayoress), Alderman W.E. Whitwell (Mayor) and Beryl Parkin.

Yard 65, Stramongate. These properties were demolished to make way for offices for the Provincial insurance company.

Toll Bar Cottage, north of Kendal, 1953. Here the road divided for Bowness and Windermere. The cottage was demolished when the Plumgarths roundabout was constructed at the end of the Kendal bypass.

The Blue Triangle juniors of the YWCA at the town hall entrance, September 1952. These girls are collecting, with a suction-assisted elephant's trunk, for the Lynmouth flood victims.

Westmorland County Hospital. The first hospital in Kendal was built in memory of Mrs James Cropper in 1876 at the top of the Captain French Lane. This was closed when the Westmorland County Hospital was opened in 1908. In 1991 the General Hospital was built on Burton Road and the old hospital was demolished. A very attractive private nursing home has been built on the site, incorporating several features of the old hospital. The original memorial hospital was the Pathology Laboratory for many years but is now Playmates day nursery.

Alderman and Mrs Bindloss. These were two of Kendal's benefactors and were particularly generous when the town hall was extended in the 1890s. Mrs Bindloss laid the foundation stone. They contributed £7,000 towards the cost of the alterations and improvements, and £3,000 for the purchase of a carillon (chime of bells) for the clock tower. Unfortunately she died before the work was completed. They also gave £30,000 towards the £80,000 cost of purchasing the Kendal Union Gas and Water Company. These were vast sums at the time.

The town crier. He was an important official before the arrival of the radio. He toured the town announcing important items of news.

AROUND KENDAL

HRH Princess Louise Augusta of Schleswig-Holstein, arriving at Heversham Station, 1907. Also on the platform are Alfred Aslett, general manager of the Furness Railway, and the Earl of Lonsdale (left).

Postmen about to set off with the morning delivery, Staveley. Many country post offices were in delightful surroundings and the next eight photographs show post offices in the villages around Kendal.

Staveley, 1915. The sign above the door says: 'Post Office for Money Orders, Savings Bank, Parcel Post Telegraph, Insurance and Annuity Business.'

Bowland Bridge post office.

Post office, Winster, Westmorland.

Underbarrow post office, 1905. The post office also served as a grocer and meal and flour dealer.

Levens post office, which served as a grocer and provision dealer.

Endmoor post office. The sign is nearly covered with ivy.

Crosthwaite post office.

Horse-drawn coach parties touring the Lyth Valley calling at the Hare and Hounds at Bowland Bridge for refreshments.

A coach party from the Commercial Livery Stables in Kendal stop at the Mason's Arms, Strawberry Bank, for refreshments.

Girls outside Cropper's paper mills, Burneside.

Junction Cottages, Burneside. These cottages have not changed, but the main road to the village on the left has been improved and now has houses on both sides.

Miss Cropper, the daughter of the owner of the Burneside paper mills, and her bridesmaids going to St Oswald's Church for her wedding, 1905.

Hollins Row, Burneside. This view has changed very little.

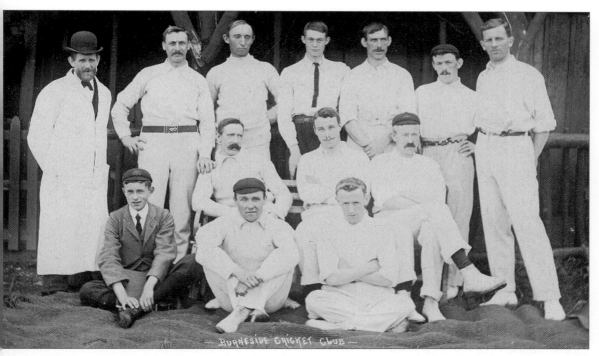

Burneside cricket team. Burneside has always had a strong village cricket team with an excellent ground.

Burneside Cricket Club pavilion.

Kendal Co-operative Society. The society had branches in all of the villages around Kendal. It had to give way to the big supermarkets, and this shop in Endmoor is now an antique dealers.

The Friends Sunday School, Preston Patrick. Children and parents are assembled for the annual Sunday School tea party.

The Staveley Branch of the Kendal Co-operative Society, 1911. The handcarts were used for local deliveries.

Looking south down Main Street, Staveley, 1906. George Sill was the landlord of the Duke William Hotel (left).

Crook School. The young teacher on the right is Edith Hutchinson. She was a keen motor cyclist and her husband was one of the founder members of the Westmorland Motor Cycle Club in 1910.

The Levens Hotel. This was a well-known stopping place on the A6 about 5 miles south of Kendal between the two wars. It was closed after the Second World War and is now a convent, occupied by the Salesian Sisters of St John Bosco and known as Brettargh Holt.